BOOBS R Brilliant

"Lots of women who might decide to breastfeed
their babies are put off by rumours and myths.
I felt that if we could tackle some of those issues
in a light-hearted way, then more women would
have the confidence to opt for breastfeeding."

Val Finigan

# Saggy BOOBS

## and other breastfeeding MYTHS

Written by Valerie Finigan

Embroidered illustration by Lou Gardiner

pinter & martin

Saggy Boobs and Other Breastfeeding Myths

First published by Lime 2008
This revised edition published by Pinter & Martin Ltd 2009
reprinted 2010

Text and design copyright © 2008 The Pennine Acute Hospitals NHS Trust
Illustrations copyright © 2008/2009 Louise Gardiner

ISBN 978-1-905177-23-3

British Library Cataloguing-in-Publication Data
A catalogue record for this book is available from the British Library

Set in Garamond

Printed in the UK by Thomson Litho, Glasgow, Scotland

This book has been printed on paper that is sourced and harvested from
sustainable forests and is FSC accredited

Copies are available at special rates for bulk orders –
contact Pinter & Martin for further details

Pinter & Martin Ltd
6 Effra Parade
London SW2 1PS

www.pinterandmartin.com

## About this book

Saggy Boobs and other Breastfeeding Myths began as an idea by Val Finigan, infant-feeding coordinator for the Pennine Acute Hospitals NHS Trust. Val wanted to work with mums and breastfeeding groups to create a fun and accessible book aimed at dispelling breastfeeding myths and encouraging more women to give their babies the best possible start by breastfeeding.

Working with Rob Vale, arts coordinator for Lime, funding for the project was successfully obtained from Awards for All. The remarkable embroidery artist Lou Gardiner was commissioned to work directly with breastfeeding support groups, collecting their views on breastfeeding myths and misnomers. Sessions were run right across the Pennine Acute Trust area, to include as wide a range of participants as possible.

These sessions led to the production of an exhibition of Lou's unique and amusing artworks and resulted in this book, which was first produced as a limited edition in 2008.

This revised edition is published by Pinter & Martin Publishers.

**Myth** Bottle-fed babies gain weight more quickly; they are fatter, chubby and cute.

## FACT

Evidence suggests that bottle-fed babies are heavier than breastfed babies at one year of age, but the weight they gain is not healthy.

Studies show that breastfed babies who control their own feeding patterns and intake tend to take just the right amount of milk needed. . Formula feeding, early introduction of solid foods, and not breastfeeding on demand, have all been implicated in risk of obesity later in life.

**Myth**

You don't ever know how much milk the baby is taking when she breastfeeds. With a bottle you can measure the amount.

**Fact**

This isn't true. There is no easy way to measure how much milk a breastfed baby takes (and it is also not necessary), but you can estimate that she is taking enough. If your baby feeds in a deep rhythmical suckling pattern with pauses and swallowing and feeding is comfortable, then she is taking plenty of milk.

From the fourth to fifth day of life, a breastfed baby will have six or more wet nappies with pale urine per day and will produce soft yellowy stools; again this indicates enough milk is being taken. Your baby will be content between feeds.

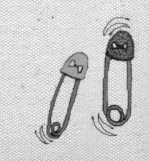

## Myth

Breastfeeding makes your boobs saggy; it ruins the shape of your breasts.

*fact*

This is simply not true. When a woman becomes pregnant, the hormones involved in sustaining her pregnancy cause permanent changes within her breasts.

Even if the pregnancy does not continue, her breasts will never be the same as they were before pregnancy. So it isn't breastfeeding that alters breast shape, size and look — it is pregnancy.

*Myth*   Bottle-fed babies sleep better and for longer than breastfed babies.

*fact*

Research suggests that bottle-fed babies may sleep for longer periods, but they don't have a better quality of sleep than breastfed babies. Formula milk is harder to digest and stays in the baby's system for longer, so it begins to ferment and this means that you will have much smellier and bulkier nappies.

Breastfed babies typically begin to sleep for longer periods of time after four weeks of life and by this time it is estimated that they sleep for the same time period as the bottle-fed baby.

All babies are uniquely wired from birth to feed, sleep and enjoy periods of wakefulness. Each baby will have his or her own unique pattern of wakefulness dependent upon on his or her own needs for feeding, comforting and loving. Whether babies are breastfed or bottle-fed formula milks, this unique pattern will occur. Some bottle-fed babies may also feed frequently and on demand.

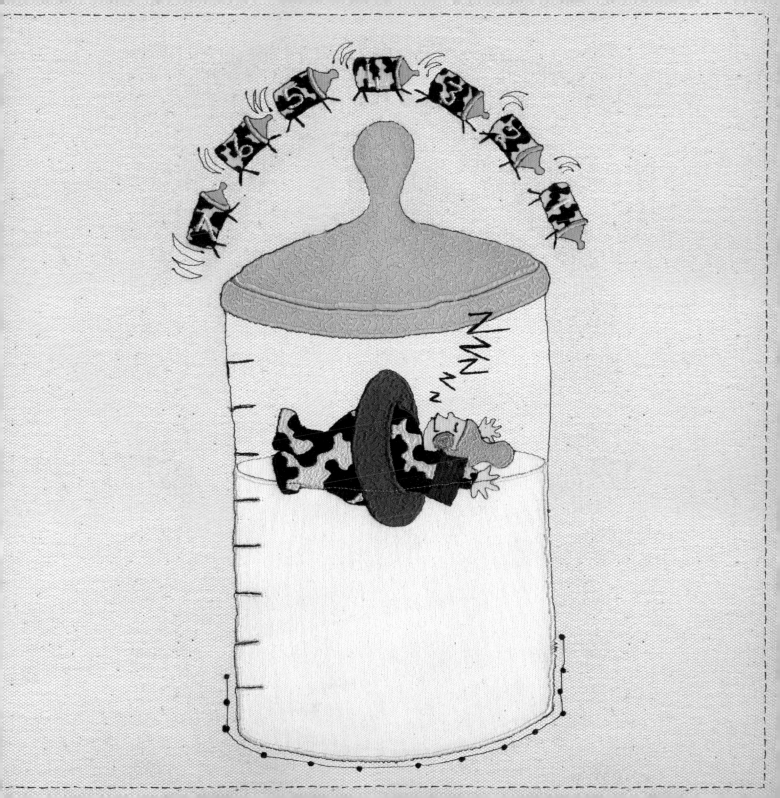

**Myth** You lose your identity breastfeeding – you're just a milk-making machine.

**Fact** While it is easy to feel like this in the early days, when your baby's needs are very demanding, this diminishes over time.

Breastfeeding takes commitment, but it strengthens the bonds with your baby and lays the foundations for his health and well-being.

**MYTH**

Oh no! Breastfeeding in public is humiliating. It's indecent.

**FACT**

Not true, rather it is the lack of public support for breastfeeding that is an issue and is indecent. It is natural and right for a mother to feel comfortable and confident that she and her baby can feed wherever and whenever they want to. Many local shops are supporting this and display the 'welcome to breastfeed here' sign.

**You are welcome to breastfeed here**

If you would prefer privacy, please ask a member of staff

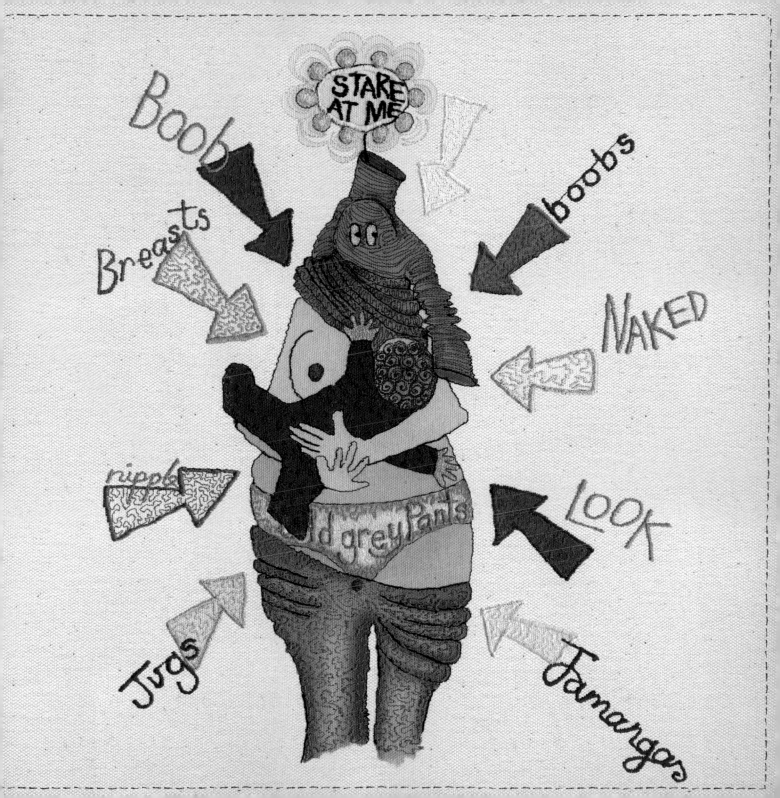

## *Myth*

Breastfeeding ties you down. Babies are like alarm clocks: they continually disturb you and demand your time.

## FACT

Yes, breastfed babies rely on their mother for nourishment and love. This doesn't mean you have to stay tied to the house: it's easy to take your breastfed baby out to the park, shopping or to visit friends. With breastfeeding your milk is readily made and you don't need to take bottles, powdered milk and water with you to feed your baby. You just need a seat and breastfeeding can be done discreetly.

Babies' needs are very intense in the early days of feeding, but this diminishes over time.

**Myth** Modern formula milks are as good as breastmilk.

**fact**

Even though modern milks are considerably better than old-fashioned milks they do not replicate breastmilk. They contain no antibodies to fight infections, no living cells, no enzymes and no hormones. They contain higher levels of aluminium, manganese, cadmium, lead and iron than breastmilk. They have significantly higher levels of protein than breastmilk, and the proteins and fats are fundamentally different from those found in breastmilk.

The constituents of formula do not change feed-to-feed, day-to-day like breastmilk and are not species specific. All we can say about formula milk is that it is successful at making babies grow well.

Formula milk, bottles and teats can cost a lot of money – between £400 and £500 a year!

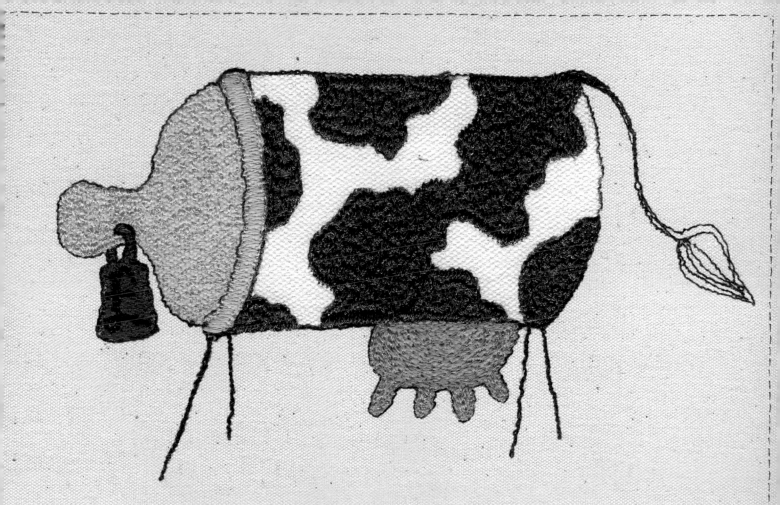

A bottle-fed baby is:

 times more likely to go into hospital with diarrhoea,
times more likely to be hospitalised with a chest infection,
times more likely to have a middle-ear infection,
times more likely to have an infection in its urine,
times more likely to develop asthma, eczema or insulin-dependent diabetes.

**Myth**

There is no difference between
a bottle-fed and a breastfed baby.

*fact*

Not true. Breastfed babies are fitter; they have higher
levels of immunity so they are less likely to become
ill. They lay down different types of fat stores and
are less likely to become obese. They are at lower risk
of developing asthma, eczema and diabetes if they
are from an allergic family.

Research has shown that they have better
cognitive development at pre-school age than
bottle-fed babies, even when factors such as parental
stimulation are accounted for.

## Myth

Breastfed babies are wooseys — they want picking up all of the time.

## Fact

Evidence suggests that breastfed babies are secure and content. They spend lots of time in close contact with their mothers and this helps their brain development. Mothers report they feel more confident in caring for their babies and can respond to their needs for love, comfort, food and security. Skin contact is good whether you breastfeed or bottle-feed your baby.

Boob →

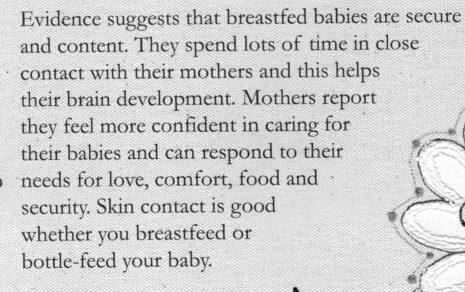

**Myth**

There is no difference in the poo of a breastfed and bottle-fed baby.

## FACT

Breastfed babies produce less waste and their nappies aren't as smelly. The baby takes just what she needs from her mother so she is less likely to gain too much weight. Bottle-fed babies' stools are much more smelly and bulky because they have more waste products. The formula milk is harder to digest and therefore stays in the stomach fermenting for a longer period of time.

**Myth**

It's not normal to breastfeed and expressing makes you feel like a cow!

*fact*

Breastfeeding is the most natural instinct in mothers throughout the world. Hormones are released during breastfeeding that encourage mother and baby attachment. Studies have shown that the close skin contact between mother and baby during breastfeeds enhances brain development.

Babies are uniquely wired from birth to breastfeed and if they are placed on their mother's abdomen following birth they will crawl to the breast and attach themselves and feed.

Expressing milk once you have established breastfeeding is useful. For example if you want time away from your baby or when you are ready to return to work. You don't have to use a pump – hand expression is more natural, gentle and can be done anywhere.

**Myth**

Breastfeeding
is difficult.

**fact**

Breastfeeding is as old as the earth. We have just lost the art
and skill of doing it. With a little support and knowledge
almost all women can breastfeed.

FEEDING TIMES
Monday x 10. 6oz
Tuesday 5.4 5 6
Wednesday x 12
Thursday x 10
Friday 8 9 10 12
Saturday
Sunday 8 10 12
Drink More
BooBs R 4 Whoozies
1 2 3 4 5 6 7 8
Quota

*Myth*

Routine and scheduled feedings are what babies need.

*fact*

Babies have their own routines. In the early weeks of life they are meant to feed frequently, but usually after six weeks of life, there is no difference in the time a breastfed baby sleeps in comparison to the amount of time a bottle-fed baby sleeps. Baby-led feedings enable your baby to take what he needs for growth and development. It also enables your baby to have a close nurturing relationship with you.

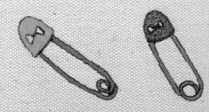

 Positioning and attaching a baby for feeds is just too difficult.

FACT Breastfeeding is a learnt skill; it takes time and a little patience at first. Getting help prior to feeding is useful, for example attending a workshop or breastfeeding group during your pregnancy.

Once you understand breastfeeding and the principles you'll be able to feed your baby in any position and anywhere.

_Myth_

You have to be available all the time — breastmilk can't be stored.

_fact_

Breastmilk is a living substance — it has cells in it that eat bacteria — so it has a long shelf life.

Breastmilk will keep at room temperature in a sterile container for 6–8 hours.

In a fridge (4–10 degrees centigrade) for 48 hours on the middle shelf.

In a fridge (less than 4 degrees centigrade) for 5–8 days.

In a freezer for 3 months or in a deep freezer for 6 months.

Being able to store breastmilk in this way enables you to leave your baby with someone else if you need to.

**Myth** It's easier and more convenient to bottle-feed.

**Fact** It's not true; it's harder to bottle-feed and even inconvenient. Formula milk must be made fresh just as baby is ready to feed. This means that you have to carry powdered milk in a container, bottles that are sterilised, and have access to boiled water whenever you go out.

Formula milk cost lots of money (around £400 per year) and bottles and teats are also costly – so you save money and have fewer things to carry when you breastfeed.

And breastfeeding is environmentally friendly: your breastmilk is beautifully packaged with no bad effects on the environment from its distribution, its packaging, or its disposal.

MYTH

When you breastfeed,
you can do nothing
but breastfeed.

# fact

Not true. Many breastfeeding women multi-task doing other jobs while feeding. Breastfeeding saves time as they don't have to make bottles or clean them up afterwards. The milk is readily available for the baby whenever or wherever the baby wants – so breastfed babies are more content as they don't have to wait while the milk is made and warmed up.

Myth — Your boobs have to be perfect to breastfeed: not too big, not too small and your nipples can't be flat.

Breast Feeding Academy

Too Big    Too Pointy    Too Small

# FACT

The size and shape of your breast is irrelevant. If your baby is positioned to suit your size and shape of breast, she will feed well and you will find feeding is comfortable. Women with flat or inverted (folded inwards) nipples often think they can't breastfeed, but babies feed from a mouthful of areola (the dark pigmented area that surrounds the nipple) not from the nipple itself.

It can sometimes take a little perseverance to get the baby to latch with a true inverted nipple, but you can ask for help and support from your midwife or a breastfeeding counsellor.

Cost a fortune

Droopy

You have to stop breastfeeding in order
to return to work – so why start?

## *Fact*

The choice to continue to breastfeed, to partially breastfeed or to stop is the mother's. European guidelines are available that support mothers in returning to work while continuing to feed.

Employers have a responsibility to provide a comfortable and private area for expressing your milk or to negotiate time to breastfeed your infant if she is close by.

Ask your midwife, a breastfeeding counsellor or health visitor about your rights. There is no better way to leave for or return from work than cuddling your infant close to you and breastfeeding.

## Mums and babies

Jen Whitworth and Elsa
Joanne Fillingham and James
Justine Hewitt and Emma
Caralyn Plowright and Jack
Vanessa Procter and Lara
**Lauren Bartlett and Joshua**
Deborah Parkinson and Georgina
Suzanne Johnson and Isabel
Pamela Urmson
Suzanne Thorp and Oscar
Ruth Hanley and Hannah
Leanne Terry and Harry
Caroline Hobson and Harry
Janette Watson and Daisy
Michelle Sager and Myles
Donna Grundy and Robert
Naheed Kauser and Saira Yurus
Ergeniya Crewe, William and Elizabeth
Elizabeth Donelly and Mathew
Louisa Kershaw and Eri
**Kathy (Health Facilitator)**
Wendy Morland (Health visitor)
Shafron Schofield and Niahl

Lisa Gee and Gabrielle
Joanne Keish and Lewis
Bev Carter and Ella
Tracey (health advisor)
Danielle Smith, Misha, and Chris
Lesley Ibbotson and Olive
Lauren Mcnamara and Kaia
Beverley Kenyon
Jenni Hyde and Anne
Sinead Hoogenbery
Jessica Wall and Ottilie
Jenny Ruff and Katy
**Jayne Brockbank and Nathan**
Laura Lopert and Sheriff and Aucia
Catherine Symons and Jack
Michelle Humphreys and Penny
Hilda Thorbjornson
Natalie Lofthaise and Hannah
Angela Collinge and George
Kerry Smith, Joshua and Isaac
Sally Moore and James
Jackie Horrits
and everyone else who took part...
thank you

This project came about through the partnership of Rob Vale, arts projects manager for Lime, and Val Finigan, infant-feeding co-ordinator for the Pennine Acute Hospitals NHS Trust.

Many thanks to all the mums, dads, babies and staff who contributed to this project.

For more information on Lou Gardiner and her weird and wonderful world of stitched characters and creatures visit her website at www.lougardiner.co.uk

Lime works in partnership with healthcare trusts to embed creativity into the health and well-being of all through arts and cultural practice. To learn more see www.limeart.org

This edition is published by Pinter & Martin Publishers, who specialise in pregnancy, childbirth and parenting titles. Visit www.pinterandmartin.com for more information.

UK National Breastfeeding Helpline 0300 100 0212

The Pennine Acute Hospitals NHS Trust

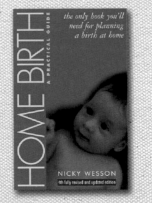

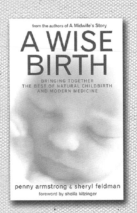